From Solo to Successful:

A Guide for Digital Solopreneurs

Solo Biz Pulse

Introduction

Definition of Solopreneurship

Solopreneurship is a business model that has gained popularity in recent years, particularly in the digital space. A solopreneur is an entrepreneur who runs their business alone. They are self-employed and work without any employees or assistance, managing all aspects of their business themselves. Solopreneurs are often freelancers, consultants, or small business owners who operate on a limited budget, but they have a unique advantage in terms of flexibility and autonomy.

Solopreneurs are responsible for every aspect of their business, from marketing and sales to administration and customer service. They are often experts in their field, and they leverage their skills and knowledge to deliver high-quality services or products. Solopreneurs are not limited to any specific industry or niche. They can be writers, designers, coaches, programmers, or any other profession that can be offered as a service or product.

Digital solopreneurs, in particular, have a distinct advantage because they can leverage the power of the internet to reach a global audience. They can market their services or products online, create digital products, and use social media and other digital tools to connect with clients and customers. Digital solopreneurs can work from anywhere in the world, as long as they have an internet connection, which makes it an ideal business model for those who value flexibility and freedom.

Solopreneurship is not for everyone, as it requires a high level of self-motivation, discipline, and resilience. Solopreneurs must be able to manage their time effectively, set goals, and prioritize tasks. They must also be comfortable with risk-taking, as they are solely responsible for the success or failure of their business.

In conclusion, solopreneurship is a business model that allows individuals to work independently and run their business on their own. It offers flexibility, autonomy, and the ability to leverage digital tools to reach a global audience. Solopreneurship requires a high level of self-motivation, discipline, and resilience, but it can be a rewarding and fulfilling career path for those who are passionate about their work and value freedom and flexibility.

Why Digital Solopreneurship is Important

In today's digital age, solopreneurship has become more important than ever before. With the rise of technology and the internet, it is now easier than ever before for individuals to start and run their own businesses. This has given rise to a new breed of entrepreneurs – the digital solopreneur.

Digital solopreneurship is important for several reasons. Firstly, it allows individuals to have more control over their work and their lives. By running their own business, solopreneurs can set their own schedules, choose their own clients, and work from anywhere in the world. This level of freedom and flexibility is not typically available in traditional employment.

Secondly, digital solopreneurship allows individuals to tap into a global marketplace. With the internet, it is now possible to reach customers all over the world. This means that solopreneurs can grow their businesses much faster than they could have in the past.

Thirdly, digital solopreneurship is important because it allows individuals to pursue their passions and interests. Many people are stuck in jobs that they don't enjoy, simply because they need the money. With solopreneurship, individuals can turn their passions and interests into profitable businesses.

Finally, digital solopreneurship is important because it allows individuals to build a brand and a reputation for themselves. By providing high-quality services or products, solopreneurs can establish themselves as experts in their fields. This can lead to more opportunities for growth and success in the future.

Overall, digital solopreneurship is an important and valuable option for anyone looking to start their own business. With the right skills, tools, and mindset, anyone can become a successful digital solopreneur.

The Purpose of the Book

The purpose of this book is to provide solopreneurs and small business owners with a comprehensive guide to digital growth. As the world becomes increasingly digital, it is essential to understand the tools and strategies that can help you succeed in today's competitive marketplace. Whether you are just starting out on your entrepreneurial journey or you are looking to take your business to the next level, this book is designed to help you achieve your goals.

One of the key objectives of this book is to help solopreneurs and small business owners understand the importance of digital marketing. The world of marketing has changed dramatically in recent years, and it is now more important than ever to have a strong online presence. This book will teach you how to create a powerful digital marketing strategy that will help you attract more customers, increase your sales, and grow your business.

Another important purpose of this book is to provide solopreneurs and small business owners with practical advice and guidance on how to manage their businesses more effectively. From financial management to time management, this book covers a wide range of topics that are essential for running a successful business. You will learn how to create a business plan, set goals, and manage your finances effectively, as well as how to delegate tasks and manage your time more efficiently.

Ultimately, the purpose of this book is to help solopreneurs and small business owners achieve their goals and realize their dreams. Whether you are looking to start a new business, expand an existing one, or simply improve your skills and knowledge, this book will provide you with the tools and strategies you need to succeed. So if you are a solopreneur or small business owner with an interest in digital growth, this book is a must-read.

The Solopreneur Mindset

Self-Motivation and Discipline

As a solopreneur, you are your own boss. This means that you are responsible for your own motivation and discipline. It can be challenging to stay motivated when you are working alone, and it can be easy to get distracted by other things. However, if you want to be successful as a digital solopreneur, you need to be self-motivated and disciplined.

One of the best ways to stay motivated is to set goals for yourself. These goals should be specific, measurable, and achievable. Write them down and create a plan to achieve them. Break down your goals into smaller, more manageable tasks, and set deadlines for each task. This will help you stay focused and motivated.

Another way to stay motivated is to surround yourself with positivity. Surround yourself with people who support your goals and believe in your vision. Join a community of like-minded solopreneurs who can offer support and encouragement when you need it. Attend events and conferences where you can learn from others and network with potential clients.

Discipline is also essential for success as a digital solopreneur. You need to have the discipline to stay focused and avoid distractions. One way to do this is to create a schedule for yourself. Set aside specific times of the day for work, and stick to this schedule as much as possible. This will help you stay on track and avoid procrastination.

It's also important to take breaks and recharge your batteries. It can be tempting to work non-stop when you are your own boss, but this can lead to burnout. Take breaks throughout the day to stretch, exercise, or meditate. This will help you stay focused and productive.

In conclusion, self-motivation and discipline are essential for success as a digital solopreneur. Set goals, surround yourself with positivity, create a schedule, and take breaks to recharge. With these habits in place, you'll be able to stay motivated, focused, and productive as you grow your digital business.

Building Confidence and Resilience

As a solopreneur or small business owner, you are constantly faced with challenges and obstacles that can test your confidence and resilience. Whether it's a difficult client, a failed project, or a slow period in your business, it's important to build the mental and emotional strength necessary to overcome these challenges and keep moving forward.

Confidence is key in any business, but especially for solopreneurs who are often the sole decision-makers and representatives of their brand. Confidence can be built by focusing on your strengths, setting achievable goals, and celebrating your successes. Take the time to reflect on what you do well and what sets you apart from your competitors. Set realistic goals that challenge you but are also attainable. And when you reach those goals, celebrate your achievements and use them as motivation to continue pushing forward.

Resilience is equally important as a solopreneur or small business owner, as setbacks and failures are inevitable. Resilience can be developed by reframing failures as opportunities for growth, practicing self-care, and surrounding yourself with a supportive network. Instead of dwelling on your failures, learn from them and use them as opportunities to improve and evolve your business. Take care of yourself by prioritizing your physical and emotional health, and seek support from friends, family, or a business coach when you need it.

Another way to build both confidence and resilience is to continually educate yourself and stay up-to-date on industry trends and best practices. Attend conferences, read books and articles, and seek out mentorship from other successful solopreneurs or business owners. The more knowledge and skills you have, the more confident and adaptable you'll be in navigating the ever-changing digital landscape.

In summary, building confidence and resilience is crucial for solopreneurs and small business owners who want to succeed in the digital world. By focusing on your strengths, setting achievable goals, reframing failures as growth opportunities, practicing self-care, and continually educating yourself, you can develop the mental and emotional strength necessary to overcome challenges and thrive in your business.

Time Management and Productivity

As a solopreneur or small business owner, time management and productivity are crucial aspects of your success. With the constant demands of running a business, it can be challenging to stay on top of everything and manage your time effectively. However, with the right tools and strategies, you can improve your productivity and accomplish more in less time.

The first step in managing your time effectively is to set clear goals and prioritize your tasks. Take some time to identify your most important goals and break them down into smaller, more manageable tasks. Then, prioritize these tasks based on their importance and urgency. This will help you stay focused and ensure that you are spending your time on the most important tasks.

Another important aspect of time management is to eliminate distractions. The digital world can be full of distractions, from social media notifications to email alerts. To stay focused, consider using tools like website blockers, email filters, and time-tracking apps. These tools can help you stay on task and avoid distractions that can eat up your time.

In addition to eliminating distractions, it's also important to take breaks and recharge. Working nonstop can lead to burnout and decreased productivity. By taking breaks and giving yourself time to recharge, you can come back to your work refreshed and more productive.

Finally, consider outsourcing tasks that are not in your area of expertise or that take up too much of your time. As a solopreneur, you may feel like you have to do everything yourself, but outsourcing can be a great way to free up your time and focus on what you do best. Whether it's hiring a virtual assistant to handle administrative tasks or outsourcing your social media management, delegating tasks can help you be more productive and grow your business.

In conclusion, time management and productivity are crucial aspects of success for solopreneurs and small business owners. By setting clear goals, prioritizing tasks, eliminating distractions, taking breaks, and outsourcing tasks, you can improve your productivity and accomplish more in less time. With the right tools and strategies, you can achieve your goals and grow your business.

Creating a Winning Business Plan

Defining Your Niche and Target Audience

As a solopreneur or small business owner, it's important to define your niche and target audience to ensure that you're reaching the right people with your digital marketing efforts. Your niche is the specific area of expertise or industry that you specialize in, while your target audience is the specific group of people who are most likely to be interested in your products or services.

To define your niche, start by considering your unique skills, experiences, and passions. What sets you apart from your competitors? What do you enjoy doing? What problems can you solve for your clients or customers? Once you've identified your niche, focus on building your brand around it. This includes creating a mission statement, developing a unique selling proposition, and creating content that speaks directly to your target audience.

Speaking of target audience, it's important to understand who your ideal customer or client is. This includes demographics such as age, gender, income, and location, as well as psychographics such as interests, values, and behaviors. By understanding your target audience, you can tailor your marketing efforts to their specific needs and preferences.

One effective way to define your niche and target audience is by conducting market research. This can include surveys, focus groups, and analyzing data from social media and other online sources. By gathering information on your audience, you can gain insights into their needs and preferences, as well as identify any gaps in the market that you can fill.

Another important factor to consider when defining your niche and target audience is competition. While it's important to differentiate yourself from your competitors, it's also important to understand what they're doing well and where there may be opportunities to improve. This can include analyzing their marketing tactics, pricing strategies, and customer service.

In summary, defining your niche and target audience is essential for digital solopreneurs and small business owners. By focusing on your unique skills and experiences, conducting market research, and understanding your competition, you can build a brand that resonates with your target audience and sets you apart from the competition.

Developing a Unique Value Proposition

As a solopreneur or small business owner in the digital world, one of the most crucial aspects of your success lies in the development of a unique value proposition. A unique value proposition, also known as a UVP, is a statement that explains what sets your business apart from the competition and why potential customers should choose you over others in the market. It is a powerful tool that can help you establish a strong brand identity, attract and retain customers, and ultimately, grow your business.

To develop a unique value proposition, you need to start by understanding your target audience and their needs. Who are your ideal customers? What challenges do they face, and how can your business solve those challenges better than anyone else? Once you have a clear understanding of your audience, you can begin crafting a UVP that resonates with them.

Your UVP should be concise, clear, and compelling. It should communicate the unique benefits of your business in a way that is easily understood by your target audience. A great UVP should answer the following questions:

1. What do you offer?
2. Who is your target audience?
3. What sets you apart from the competition?
4. What are the benefits of choosing your business?

To create a compelling UVP, you should focus on the benefits of your business rather than just the features. Benefits are what your customers will ultimately care about, and they are what will motivate them to choose your business over others in the market.

Once you have developed your UVP, you should use it consistently across all of your marketing and branding efforts. Your UVP should be prominently displayed on your website, social media profiles, and any other marketing materials you use to attract and retain customers.

In conclusion, developing a unique value proposition is essential for solopreneurs and small business owners who want to establish a strong brand identity and grow their business in the digital world. By understanding your audience, focusing on the benefits of your business, and using your UVP consistently across all of your marketing efforts, you can create a compelling statement that sets your business apart from the competition and attracts and retains customers.

Setting Realistic Business Goals

As a solopreneur or small business owner, you want to grow your business and achieve success. However, in order to do so, it's important to set realistic business goals. This means taking the time to evaluate where your business is currently at and where you want it to be in the future. In this chapter, we will discuss how to set realistic business goals for digital solopreneurs and small business owners.

The first step in setting realistic business goals is to evaluate your current situation. This means taking a look at your current revenue, expenses, and customer base. Once you have a clear understanding of where you are at, you can then start to set goals for where you want to be in the future. It's important to set specific goals that are measurable, achievable, relevant, and time-bound. This means setting goals that are specific, such as increasing revenue by 10%, achievable, such as increasing your customer base by 20%, relevant, such as improving your website's user experience, and time-bound, such as achieving these goals within the next six months.

When setting your goals, it's important to be realistic. Don't set goals that are too lofty or unrealistic, as this can lead to frustration and disappointment if you are unable to achieve them. Instead, set achievable goals that will help you grow your business in a sustainable way.

Another key factor in setting realistic business goals is to prioritize them. It's important to focus on the goals that will have the biggest impact on your business. This means setting goals that are aligned with your overall business strategy and that will help you achieve your long-term objectives.

Finally, it's important to track your progress and adjust your goals as needed. This means regularly reviewing your progress towards your goals and making adjustments if necessary. This will help you stay on track and ensure that you are making progress towards achieving your business objectives.

In conclusion, setting realistic business goals is a key factor in achieving success as a digital solopreneur or small business owner. By taking the time to evaluate your current situation, setting specific and achievable goals, prioritizing them, and tracking your progress, you can set your business on a path towards growth and success.

Building Your Online Presence

Establishing a Professional Website

In today's digital age, having a professional website is crucial for any solopreneur or small business owner looking to establish an online presence. A website is a powerful tool that can help you showcase your products or services, build your brand, and connect with potential customers from all over the world.

Here are some tips for establishing a professional website:

1. Determine your website's purpose

Before building your website, it's important to determine its purpose. What do you want to achieve with your website? Is it to sell products or services? Or is it to establish a brand and build an online presence? Once you determine your website's purpose, you can start building it with that goal in mind.

2. Choose a domain name and hosting platform

Your domain name is the address of your website on the internet. It's important to choose a domain name that is easy to remember and reflects your brand. Once you have chosen your domain name, you will need to choose a hosting platform to host your website. There are many hosting platforms available, so do your research to find the one that best fits your needs and budget.

3. Choose a website builder

There are many website builders available that make it easy for even the most technologically challenged solopreneurs and small business owners to build a professional website. Some popular website builders include WordPress, Wix, and Squarespace. Each website builder has its own strengths and weaknesses, so choose the one that best fits your needs.

4. Create high-quality content

Once you have chosen your website builder, it's time to start creating content for your website. Your content should be high-quality, relevant, and engaging. This will help attract potential customers and keep them on your website for longer periods of time.

5. Optimize for search engines

Search engine optimization (SEO) is the process of optimizing your website to rank higher in search engine results pages (SERPs). This can help drive traffic to your website and increase your visibility online. Some basic SEO techniques include using relevant keywords, creating high-quality content, and optimizing your website for mobile devices.

In conclusion, establishing a professional website is essential for any solopreneur or small business owner looking to establish an online presence. By following these tips, you can create a website that reflects your brand and helps you achieve your business goals.

Optimizing Your Social Media Profiles

In today's digital age, having a strong social media presence is crucial for solopreneurs and small business owners. It's not enough to simply have a presence on social media platforms, but it's important to optimize your profiles to ensure that they are attracting the right audience and delivering the right message.

The first step in optimizing your social media profiles is to ensure that your branding is consistent across all platforms. This means using the same profile picture, cover photo, and bio on all of your social media accounts. Consistency helps establish your brand identity and makes it easier for people to recognize your business.

Next, make sure that your profiles are complete and up-to-date. This includes filling out all of the necessary information such as your website, contact information, and business hours. Incomplete profiles can make it difficult for potential customers to find and engage with your business.

Another important aspect of optimizing your social media profiles is to use keywords and hashtags that are relevant to your business. This helps improve your visibility in search results and makes it easier for people to find your business when searching for products or services in your industry.

It's also important to engage with your audience on social media. This means responding to comments and messages, sharing relevant content, and posting regularly. Engaging with your audience helps build relationships and establishes your business as a trusted source of information in your industry.

Finally, track your social media analytics to see what's working and what's not. This includes monitoring your follower count, engagement rates, and referral traffic to your website. Analyzing your social media data can help you make informed decisions about your social media strategy and adjust your approach as needed.

By optimizing your social media profiles, you can attract the right audience, build relationships with your followers, and ultimately grow your business online.

Creating Content that Engages Your Audience

In today's digital age, creating content that engages your audience is crucial for the success of your business. With the rise of social media and other digital platforms, it's now more important than ever to produce content that not only attracts your target audience but also keeps them engaged and interested in what you have to offer.

As a solopreneur or small business owner, creating engaging content can be challenging, but it's not impossible. Here are some tips to help you create content that captures your audience's attention and keeps them coming back for more.

1. Know Your Audience

The first step in creating engaging content is to know your audience. Who are they? What are their interests? What challenges do they face? By understanding your audience, you can create content that resonates with them and addresses their needs.

2. Be Authentic

Authenticity is key when it comes to creating engaging content. Your audience wants to connect with you on a personal level, and they can tell when you're not being genuine. Be yourself, share your story, and show your audience who you are. This will help you build trust and establish a connection with your audience.

3. Use Visuals

Visuals are a powerful way to engage your audience. Use high-quality images, videos, and graphics to make your content more appealing and easy to consume. Visuals can also help you convey your message more effectively and make your content more memorable.

4. Keep it Simple

When it comes to creating engaging content, simplicity is key. Keep your content simple, easy to understand, and to the point. Your audience is busy, and they don't have time to read through lengthy articles or watch long videos. Keep your content concise and straightforward.

5. Be Consistent

Consistency is essential when it comes to creating engaging content. Your audience wants to know what to expect from you, so make sure you're consistent in your messaging, tone, and frequency of content. This will help you establish a strong brand identity and build trust with your audience.

In conclusion, creating engaging content is essential for the success of your business in today's digital age. By knowing your audience, being authentic, using visuals, keeping it simple, and being consistent, you can create content that attracts and engages your audience, ultimately leading to increased brand awareness, customer loyalty, and business growth.

Digital Marketing Strategies for Solopreneurs

Search Engine Optimization (SEO)

Search Engine Optimization (SEO) is a vital aspect of digital marketing that solopreneurs and small business owners should consider if they want to increase their online visibility and drive more traffic to their websites. SEO is a technique that involves optimizing your website to rank higher in search engine results pages (SERPs) for relevant keywords and phrases. It involves a combination of on-page optimization, off-page optimization, and technical optimization.

On-page optimization involves optimizing your website's content, structure, and HTML code to make it more search engine friendly. This includes optimizing your titles, meta descriptions, headings, and content for relevant keywords and phrases. You should also ensure that your website is easy to navigate, has a clear structure, and is mobile-friendly.

Off-page optimization involves building high-quality backlinks to your website from other relevant and authoritative websites. This can be done through guest blogging, social media marketing, and influencer outreach. The more high-quality backlinks you have, the higher your website will rank in SERPs.

Technical optimization involves optimizing your website's technical aspects, such as page speed, mobile-friendliness, and website security. This can be achieved by optimizing your website's images, compressing your website's code, and using secure hosting.

SEO is a long-term strategy that requires consistent effort and dedication. It is not a one-time fix, but rather an ongoing process that requires continuous optimization and refinement. However, the benefits of SEO are significant, including increased online visibility, higher website traffic, and improved user engagement.

In summary, solopreneurs and small business owners with an interest in digital growth should consider incorporating SEO into their digital marketing strategy. By optimizing their website for search engines, they can increase their online visibility, drive more traffic to their website, and ultimately grow their business.

Pay-Per-Click (PPC) Advertising

Pay-per-click (PPC) advertising is a digital marketing strategy that allows advertisers to place ads on search engines or other websites and only pay when someone clicks on their ad. This method of advertising is popular with solopreneurs and small business owners because it can be affordable, measurable, and effective.

To get started with PPC advertising, you first need to choose a platform. Google Ads is the most popular platform for PPC advertising, but there are other options like Bing Ads, Facebook Ads, and LinkedIn Ads. Once you have chosen a platform, you need to create an account and set a budget for your ads.

The next step is to create your ads. Your ads should be relevant, engaging, and have a clear call-to-action. You should also choose keywords that are relevant to your business and target your ads to specific locations and demographics.

One of the benefits of PPC advertising is that you can track the performance of your ads in real-time. You can see how many clicks your ads are getting, how much you are paying per click, and how much revenue you are generating from your ads. This data can help you make informed decisions about your advertising strategy and adjust your budget and targeting as needed.

PPC advertising can be a cost-effective way to drive traffic to your website and generate leads for your business. However, it is important to remember that PPC advertising is not a one-size-fits-all solution. Your success with PPC advertising will depend on your industry, your target audience, and your marketing goals.

Overall, PPC advertising can be a valuable tool for solopreneurs and small business owners who want to grow their business online. By choosing the right platform, creating engaging ads, and tracking your results, you can use PPC advertising to reach new customers and drive sales for your business.

Email Marketing

Email marketing is one of the most effective ways to reach your target audience and promote your products or services. It allows you to connect with your customers and build a relationship with them, leading to increased loyalty and repeat business. For solopreneurs and small business owners, email marketing can be a powerful tool for digital growth.

To get started with email marketing, you first need to build a list of subscribers. This can be done by offering a lead magnet, such as a free eBook or webinar, in exchange for a visitor's email address. You can also add a subscription form to your website and social media pages to encourage sign-ups.

Once you have a list of subscribers, you can start sending them emails. It's important to keep your emails relevant and valuable to your audience. This means sending targeted messages based on their interests and needs. You can segment your list based on factors such as past purchases, website behavior, and demographics to ensure your emails are personalized and effective.

In addition to promotional emails, you can also send newsletters and updates to keep your subscribers engaged and informed. This can include industry news, company updates, and exclusive offers. Be sure to include a clear call-to-action in each email, such as a link to a product page or a request to follow you on social media.

To ensure the success of your email marketing campaigns, it's important to track your results. This includes monitoring open rates, click-through rates, and conversion rates. You can use this data to refine your strategy and improve your future emails.

Overall, email marketing is a valuable tool for solopreneurs and small business owners looking to grow their digital presence. By building a list of subscribers and sending targeted, valuable emails, you can build relationships with your customers and drive sales for your business.

Building a Strong Brand Identity

Crafting Your Brand Story

As a solopreneur or small business owner, you are the face and voice of your brand. Crafting a compelling brand story is crucial to creating a strong and memorable brand identity that resonates with your target audience. Your brand story should communicate who you are, what you do, and why you do it.

The first step in crafting your brand story is to define your brand values. What are the core values that guide your business? What do you stand for? Your values should be the foundation of your brand story and should be reflected in everything you do. Your brand values will help you connect with your audience on a deeper level and build trust and loyalty.

Once you have defined your brand values, it's time to create your brand narrative. Your brand narrative should be a compelling and engaging story that communicates your brand values and connects with your audience emotionally. Your brand narrative should answer the following questions:

- Who are you and what do you do?
- What are your brand values and why are they important to

you?

- How do your products or services solve your audience's problems?
- What is your brand's unique selling proposition?
- What is your vision for the future?

Your brand narrative should be consistent across all your marketing channels, from your website to your social media profiles. Your brand narrative should also be authentic and honest. Don't try to be someone you're not or pretend to be bigger than you are. Your audience will appreciate honesty and authenticity.

Finally, once you have crafted your brand story, it's time to share it with the world. Use your brand story as the foundation for all your marketing efforts. Use it to create compelling content, develop your brand voice and tone, and engage with your audience on social media. Your brand story should be the driving force behind everything you do.

In conclusion, crafting your brand story is crucial to creating a strong and memorable brand identity that resonates with your target audience. Define your brand values, create a compelling brand narrative, and share it with the world. Your brand story will help you connect with your audience on a deeper level and build trust and loyalty.

Creating a Memorable Logo and Branding Materials

As a digital solopreneur or small business owner, your brand is your identity. It is what sets you apart from the competition and makes you recognizable to your target audience. Your logo and branding materials are at the forefront of your brand, and they play a critical role in how people perceive your business. Therefore, it is essential to create a memorable logo and branding materials that represent your brand accurately.

The first step in creating a memorable logo is to understand your brand identity. Consider what your business stands for, your values, and your target audience. This will help you create a logo that authentically represents your brand. Choose a color scheme that aligns with your brand identity and evokes the emotions you want your audience to feel when they see your logo.

Once you have created your logo, it is time to develop your branding materials. Your branding materials should include your website, business cards, social media profiles, and any other marketing materials you use to promote your business. Consistency is key when it comes to branding, so make sure that all your materials share the same color scheme, typography, and overall design aesthetic.

When designing your branding materials, keep your audience in mind. Consider their preferences, behaviors, and what they find appealing. Your branding should not only represent your business, but it should also resonate with your audience.

In addition to creating a memorable logo and branding materials, it is also essential to protect your brand. Trademarking your logo and business name can prevent others from using it and help you avoid legal issues down the line. It is also important to monitor your brand online and address any negative feedback or reviews promptly.

In conclusion, creating a memorable logo and branding materials is a crucial step in building a successful digital business. By understanding your brand identity, developing consistent branding, and protecting your brand, you can establish a strong presence in your industry and attract your target audience.

Consistency in Branding Across All Channels

One of the most important aspects of building a strong brand is consistency. It's not just about having a great logo or a catchy tagline – it's about making sure that your brand is recognizable and consistent across all channels.

As a solopreneur or small business owner, your brand is your identity. It's what sets you apart from your competitors and helps you stand out in a crowded market. But building a strong brand takes time and effort, and it requires a lot of attention to detail.

One of the biggest challenges that solopreneurs and small business owners face when it comes to branding is maintaining consistency across all channels. This means ensuring that your brand messaging, visual identity, and tone of voice are consistent across all of your marketing channels, from your website and social media to your email marketing campaigns and offline marketing materials.

Here are some tips for maintaining consistency in your branding across all channels:

1. Develop a brand style guide: A brand style guide is a document that outlines the guidelines for how your brand

should be presented across all channels. It should include your brand messaging, visual identity, tone of voice, and any other guidelines that are important to your brand.

2. Use consistent visuals: Your visual identity is a crucial part of your brand. Make sure that your logo, color scheme, typography, and other visual elements are consistent across all channels.

3. Maintain a consistent tone of voice: Your brand's tone of voice is the personality of your brand. It's how you communicate with your audience and how you make them feel. Make sure that your tone of voice is consistent across all channels.

4. Be consistent in your messaging: Your brand messaging is the story that you tell about your brand. Make sure that your messaging is consistent across all channels, and that you are communicating the same message to your audience regardless of where they are interacting with your brand.

By maintaining consistency in your branding across all channels, you will build a stronger, more recognizable brand that will help you stand out in your market. It takes time and effort, but it's worth it in the end.

Managing Finances as a Solopreneur

Setting Up a Bookkeeping System

One of the most crucial aspects of running a successful business is maintaining accurate financial records. As a solopreneur or small business owner, you need to have a bookkeeping system in place to track your income and expenses, manage your cash flow, and stay on top of your tax obligations. Here are some tips on setting up a bookkeeping system for your digital business.

1. Choose the right software

There are plenty of bookkeeping software options available, both free and paid. Some popular ones include QuickBooks, Xero, FreshBooks, and Wave. Look for software that suits your specific needs and budget. Consider factors such as ease of use, features, scalability, and integrations with other tools you use for your business.

2. Set up your accounts

Once you've chosen your software, set up your accounts by creating a chart of accounts that reflects your business structure and needs. This will help you categorize your income and expenses accurately, and make it easier to generate reports and file taxes. You may also need to set up separate bank accounts for your business to keep your personal and business finances separate.

3. Record your transactions

Now that your accounts are set up, start recording your transactions in your bookkeeping software. This includes any income you receive, such as from sales, services, or affiliate marketing, as well as any expenses you incur, such as for advertising, software subscriptions, or equipment. Be sure to categorize each transaction accurately, and keep your receipts and invoices organized.

4. Reconcile your accounts

Regularly reconcile your bank and credit card accounts to ensure that your records match your actual transactions. This will help you catch any errors or discrepancies early on, and make it easier to identify any outstanding payments or deposits.

5. Generate reports

Your bookkeeping software should allow you to generate various reports, such as profit and loss statements, balance sheets, and cash flow statements. Use these reports to monitor your financial health, identify trends, and make informed decisions about your business.

By setting up a bookkeeping system for your digital business, you'll be better equipped to manage your finances, stay compliant with tax laws, and make informed decisions about your future growth. Don't neglect this critical aspect of your business, and consider seeking professional help if needed.

Managing Cash Flow

Cash flow management is one of the most critical aspects of running a successful business. Regardless of the scale of your enterprise, you need to keep a close eye on your cash flow to ensure you don't run into financial difficulties. Cash flow is the money that flows in and out of your business, and it's essential to keep track of it to keep your business afloat.

Solopreneurs and small business owners need to manage their cash flow effectively to ensure they can cover their expenses and invest in growth opportunities. Here are some tips to help you manage your cash flow effectively:

1. Create a cash flow forecast: You need to have a clear understanding of your cash flow to make informed

decisions. Creating a cash flow forecast can help you anticipate your cash inflows and outflows, which will help you make better financial decisions.

2. Monitor your expenses: It's essential to track your expenses and avoid overspending. Look for ways to reduce your costs without compromising the quality of your products or services.

3. Invoice promptly: Make sure you send your invoices on time and follow up with your clients to ensure they pay on time. Late payments can hurt your cash flow, so it's essential to stay on top of your invoicing.

4. Negotiate payment terms: Negotiate payment terms with your clients to ensure you get paid on time. You can offer discounts for early payment or charge interest for late payment.

5. Build a cash reserve: It's essential to build a cash reserve to cover unexpected expenses or shortfalls in cash flow. You can set aside a percentage of your revenue to build your cash reserve.

6. Consider financing options: If you need to invest in growth opportunities, consider financing options such as loans or lines of credit. Make sure you understand the terms and conditions and can afford the repayments.

Managing your cash flow can be challenging, but it's essential to keep your business running smoothly. By creating a cash flow forecast, monitoring your expenses, invoicing promptly, negotiating payment terms, building a cash reserve, and considering financing options, you can manage your cash flow effectively and grow your business.

Tax Planning and Preparation

As a solopreneur, tax planning and preparation may not be at the top of your to-do list, but it's an essential part of running a successful business. Proper tax planning can help you save money, avoid penalties and fines, and ensure that you comply with all tax laws and regulations. In this subchapter, we'll cover everything you need to know about tax planning and preparation as a solopreneur.

The first step in tax planning is to understand your tax obligations. As a solopreneur, you're responsible for paying self-employment taxes, which includes Social Security and Medicare taxes. You'll also need to pay income taxes on your business profits. It's important to keep accurate records of all your income and expenses so that you can accurately calculate your taxes owed.

One of the best ways to save money on taxes is to take advantage of deductions and credits. As a solopreneur, you may be able to deduct expenses related to your business, such as home office expenses, travel expenses, and equipment purchases. You may also be eligible for tax credits, such as the Earned Income Tax Credit or the Child and Dependent Care Credit.

Another important aspect of tax planning is choosing the right business structure. Depending on your business goals and financial situation, you may benefit from setting up your business as a sole proprietorship, LLC, or S Corporation. Each business structure has its own tax implications, so it's important to choose the one that best fits your needs.

When it comes to tax preparation, it's important to stay organized throughout the year. Keep track of all your income and expenses, and make sure to file your taxes on time. You may want to consider hiring a tax professional to help you with tax preparation, especially if you have a complex tax situation.

In conclusion, tax planning and preparation are essential for solopreneurs who want to run a successful business. By understanding your tax obligations, taking advantage of deductions and credits, choosing the right business structure, and staying organized throughout the year, you can save money and avoid costly mistakes.

Building a Strong Network

Identifying Potential Partners and Collaborators

As a solopreneur or small business owner, you may have the skills and expertise needed to run your business, but you may not have all the resources and support you need to grow your business. One way to overcome this challenge is to identify potential partners and collaborators who can help you achieve your business goals.

Here are some tips for identifying potential partners and collaborators:

1. Look for businesses and individuals who share your values and goals.

When looking for potential partners and collaborators, it is important to identify businesses and individuals who share your values and goals. This will ensure that you have a strong foundation for your partnership and that you are working towards a common vision.

2. Identify businesses and individuals with complementary skills and expertise.

When partnering with other businesses and individuals, it is important to identify those with complementary skills and expertise. This will allow you to leverage each other's strengths and create a more well-rounded and effective team.

3. Research potential partners and collaborators.

Before reaching out to potential partners and collaborators, it is important to do your research. This will help you identify businesses and individuals who are a good fit for your business and who can help you achieve your goals.

4. Attend industry events and conferences.

Attending industry events and conferences is a great way to meet potential partners and collaborators. These events provide opportunities to network with other professionals in your industry and to learn about new trends and technologies.

5. Leverage social media and online communities.

Social media and online communities are great resources for connecting with potential partners and collaborators. Joining online groups and forums related to your industry can help you connect with like-minded individuals and businesses.

In conclusion, identifying potential partners and collaborators is a crucial part of growing your business as a solopreneur or small business owner. By following these tips, you can build a strong network of partners and collaborators who can help you achieve your business goals.

Attending Networking Events and Conferences

Networking events and conferences offer solopreneurs and small business owners the opportunity to connect with like-minded individuals, learn new skills, and expand their professional network. Whether you're attending a local meetup or a large industry conference, these events can be a valuable resource for your business growth.

Before attending any event, it's important to do your research. Look for events that are relevant to your niche or industry and that feature speakers or workshops that align with your business goals. Consider your budget and time constraints when selecting events, and be sure to register in advance to secure your spot.

When you arrive at the event, make an effort to introduce yourself to other attendees. Be friendly and approachable, and don't be afraid to strike up a conversation. Remember that everyone is there for the same reason – to connect with others and learn something new.

Take advantage of any networking opportunities that the event offers. Many conferences and events have designated networking sessions or social events where you can meet and mingle with other attendees. Don't be shy about exchanging business cards or contact information, and be sure to follow up with anyone you meet after the event.

Attending workshops and sessions is another great way to make the most of your time at a networking event or conference. Take notes and ask questions, and be sure to engage with the speaker and other attendees. You never know what new insights or ideas you might gain from these sessions.

Finally, don't forget to have fun! Networking events and conferences can be a great way to break out of your daily routine and meet new people. So, make the most of the experience and enjoy yourself.

In conclusion, attending networking events and conferences can be a valuable resource for solopreneurs and small business owners looking to grow their business. By doing your research, being social, taking advantage of networking opportunities, and engaging with sessions and speakers, you can make the most out of your time at these events.

Building Relationships with Influencers in Your Industry

As a solopreneur or small business owner, it can be challenging to get your brand noticed in a crowded digital space. One effective way to gain visibility and credibility is by building relationships with influencers in your industry.

Influencers are individuals who have a significant following on social media, blogs, or other digital platforms. They have the power to sway people's opinions and behavior, and partnering with them can help you reach a wider audience.

Here are some tips for building relationships with influencers:

1. Identify the Right Influencers

The first step is to identify the influencers who align with your brand and target audience. Look for individuals who have a following that overlaps with your target market and whose content aligns with your brand values. You can use tools like BuzzSumo or Hootsuite to find influencers in your industry.

2. Engage with Their Content

Once you have identified the influencers, start engaging with their content. Follow them on social media, comment on their posts, and share their content with your audience. This will help you build a relationship with them and show that you value their work.

3. Provide Value

Influencers are often inundated with requests for partnerships, so you need to provide value to stand out. Start by offering to collaborate on a piece of content or provide them with an exclusive offer for their audience. This will help you build a relationship with them and show that you are committed to creating value for their audience.

4. Be Authentic

When building relationships with influencers, it's essential to be authentic. Don't try to force a partnership or fake enthusiasm for their work. Instead, focus on building a genuine relationship based on shared values and interests.

5. Measure Results

Finally, it's essential to measure the results of your influencer partnerships. Track metrics like website traffic, social media engagement, and sales to see how your partnership is impacting your brand's growth.

In conclusion, building relationships with influencers can be a powerful way to grow your brand as a solopreneur or small business owner. By identifying the right influencers, engaging with their content, providing value, being authentic, and measuring results, you can build lasting relationships that benefit both you and the influencer.

Scaling Your Business as a Solopreneur

Hiring and Managing Freelancers

As a digital solopreneur or small business owner, there will come a time when you need to hire freelancers to help you with various aspects of your business. Freelancers are a great resource, as they can offer specialized skills and expertise without the need for a long-term commitment. However, hiring and managing freelancers requires a different approach than working with full-time employees. Here are some tips for successfully hiring and managing freelancers.

Define Your Needs

Before you start looking for freelancers, it's important to define your needs. What specific tasks do you need help with? What skills and expertise are required? What is your budget? By having a clear idea of what you need, you'll be able to find the right freelancers for the job.

Find the Right Freelancers

There are many ways to find freelancers, including job boards, social media, and referrals. When evaluating potential freelancers, look for experience and expertise that aligns with your needs. Check their portfolio and reviews to ensure they have a track record of delivering quality work.

Communicate Clearly

Effective communication is key when working with freelancers. Clearly communicate your expectations, deadlines, and any other relevant information. Make sure you're available to answer any questions and provide feedback throughout the project.

Set Clear Expectations

Setting clear expectations is important for both you and the freelancer. Be clear about the scope of the project, the timeline, and any other expectations you have. Establish a clear payment structure and make sure both parties are in agreement before starting the project.

Manage the Project

Managing the project is crucial to its success. Keep track of progress, provide feedback, and make sure the project is on track to meet the deadline. If issues arise, address them promptly to avoid any delays or misunderstandings.

Pay on Time

Paying freelancers on time is important for building trust and maintaining a positive working relationship. Make sure you have a clear payment schedule in place and stick to it.

In conclusion, hiring and managing freelancers can be a great way to grow your digital solopreneur or small business. By following these tips, you can find the right freelancers and successfully manage projects to achieve your business goals.

Automating Repetitive Tasks

As a solopreneur or small business owner, you probably have a lot on your plate, from managing your website to responding to customer inquiries. With so many tasks to handle, it can be challenging to find the time to focus on growing your business. However, there is a solution to this problem: automating repetitive tasks.

Automating repetitive tasks can save you a lot of time and energy, allowing you to focus on more important aspects of your business. Here are some examples of tasks that you can automate:

1. Email marketing: You can use email marketing tools such as Mailchimp or Constant Contact to automate your email marketing campaigns. These tools allow you to create and schedule emails in advance, so you don't have to manually send them every time.

2. Social media management: You can use social media management tools such as Hootsuite or Buffer to schedule your social media posts in advance. This way, you can maintain a consistent presence on social media without spending too much time on it.

3. Customer service: You can use chatbots or automated email responses to handle customer inquiries. This way, you can provide quick and efficient customer service without having to respond to every message manually.

4. Data entry: You can use tools such as Zapier or IFTTT to automate data entry tasks, such as adding new contacts to your email list or updating your CRM.

By automating these repetitive tasks, you can streamline your workflow and save a lot of time and energy. This will allow you to focus on more important aspects of your business, such as developing new products or services, or building relationships with your customers.

However, it is important to remember that automation is not a one-size-fits-all solution. You need to carefully evaluate which tasks can be automated and which ones require a personal touch. For example, while chatbots can be useful for handling simple customer inquiries, they cannot replace the value of a human conversation in complex situations.

In conclusion, automating repetitive tasks can be a game-changer for solopreneurs and small business owners. By doing so, you can save time and energy, allowing you to focus on growing your business. However, it is important to carefully evaluate which tasks can be automated, and which ones require a personal touch. With the right balance, automation can be a powerful tool for digital solopreneurs looking to grow their business.

Outsourcing Non-Core Functions

As a solopreneur or small business owner, you wear many hats. You're the CEO, the accountant, the marketer, the salesperson, and the customer support team, all rolled into one. It's a lot of work, and it can be overwhelming at times. But what if you could outsource some of those non-core functions to someone else?

Outsourcing can be a great way to free up your time and focus on what you do best. It can also save you money in the long run, as you'll only pay for the services you need, when you need them.

So, what kinds of non-core functions can you outsource? Here are a few examples:

1. Administrative tasks - This can include things like data entry, scheduling appointments, and bookkeeping. You can hire a virtual assistant to take care of these tasks for you.

2. Graphic design - If you need a logo, website design, or other graphic design work done, you can hire a freelance graphic designer to do it for you.

3. Social media management - If you're not a social media expert, you can hire someone to manage your social media accounts for you. They can create content, schedule posts, and engage with your audience.

4. Content creation - If you need blog posts, articles, or other content created, you can hire a freelance writer to do it for you.

When you're outsourcing, it's important to choose the right person or company for the job. Look for someone with experience in the area you need help with, and check their references and portfolio before hiring them.

It's also important to have clear communication with your outsourced team. Make sure you're both on the same page about what needs to be done, and how often. Set clear deadlines and expectations, and check in regularly to make sure everything is going smoothly.

Outsourcing can be a great way to grow your business and free up your time. Just make sure you choose the right people to work with, and communicate clearly to ensure success.

Conclusion

Recap of Key Concepts

As a solopreneur or small business owner with an interest in digital growth, you need to have a firm understanding of the key concepts that drive success in this arena. In this subchapter, we will take a moment to recap some of the most important ideas covered in this book so far.

First and foremost, we have emphasized the importance of building a strong personal brand. As a solopreneur, your brand is tightly linked to your own identity, and it is essential that you cultivate a clear and consistent message across all channels. This includes your website, social media profiles, email marketing, and any other channels you use to communicate with your audience.

Another key concept we have explored is the importance of creating valuable content. Your content is the backbone of your digital strategy, and it is what will attract and retain your audience. It is crucial to understand your audience's needs and interests and create content that speaks directly to them.

We have also discussed the importance of building an engaged community around your brand. This means fostering relationships with your audience through active engagement, responding to comments and messages, and creating a sense of community among your followers. This can be achieved through social media, email marketing, or even in-person events.

Finally, we have explored the importance of leveraging data to optimize your digital strategy. This means tracking and analyzing metrics like website traffic, social media engagement, and email open rates to understand what is working and what is not. By using this data to make informed decisions, you can continuously improve and refine your strategy over time.

In summary, as a solopreneur or small business owner with an interest in digital growth, it is essential to focus on building a strong personal brand, creating valuable content, fostering an engaged community, and leveraging data to optimize your strategy. By keeping these key concepts in mind and continuously refining your approach, you can achieve success as a digital solopreneur.

Final Words of Encouragement

As a solopreneur or small business owner, you have embarked on a journey that requires courage, dedication, and perseverance. The path to success is never easy, but with the right mindset, strategies, and support, you can achieve your goals and create a fulfilling and prosperous digital business.

In this book, we have explored various aspects of digital entrepreneurship, from identifying your niche and target audience to building your brand, creating content, and leveraging social media and other digital channels to reach and engage your customers. We have also discussed the importance of mindset, self-care, and continuous learning in the digital age.

Now, as you reach the end of this book, I want to offer you some final words of encouragement to help you stay focused, motivated, and inspired on your journey.

Firstly, remember that success is not a destination but a journey. It's not about achieving a certain level of income, recognition, or status, but about enjoying the process of growth, learning, and contribution. Embrace the challenges, failures, and setbacks as opportunities to learn, improve, and innovate.

Secondly, surround yourself with positive and supportive people who believe in your vision, values, and potential. Join online communities, attend events, and connect with mentors, peers, and customers who share your passion and mission. Collaboration and feedback are essential for growth and innovation.

Thirdly, stay true to your values, purpose, and vision. Don't compromise your integrity, creativity, or authenticity for short-term gains or popularity. Your unique voice, perspective, and personality are your most valuable assets in the digital world.

Finally, take care of yourself, both physically and mentally. Digital entrepreneurship can be demanding and stressful, but it can also be fulfilling and empowering. Prioritize your health, relationships, and personal growth. Celebrate your achievements, learn from your mistakes, and keep moving forward with passion, purpose, and resilience.

Thank you for reading this book and joining the digital solopreneurship revolution. I wish you all the best in your journey to success and fulfillment. Remember, you are not alone, and your dreams are within reach.

Resources for Continued Growth and Learning.

As a solopreneur, the journey to success is a continuous learning process. You must stay on top of trends and continuously improve yourself to remain relevant in the fast-paced digital world. Fortunately, there are several resources available to help you continue your growth and learning.

1. Online Courses- There are several online courses available that can help you learn new skills or improve existing ones. Platforms like Udemy, Coursera, and Skillshare offer a wide range of courses in different niches.

You can learn about social media marketing, email marketing, SEO, web development, graphic design and many more. These courses are usually affordable and sometimes free, so you can choose the ones that work for you and your budget.

2. Webinars – Webinars are an excellent way to learn from experts in your industry. They are usually free and conducted online, making it easy for you to attend from anywhere. You can attend webinars on different topics and learn from experienced professionals. You can also participate in live Q&A sessions and get your questions answered.

3. Podcasts – Podcasts are an excellent way to learn while you are on the go. You can listen to podcasts while commuting, exercising, or doing other activities. Many podcasts offer valuable insights and tips on different topics, from entrepreneurship to marketing, and technology. Some popular podcasts for solopreneurs include The Tim Ferriss Show, The GaryVee Audio Experience, and The Smart Passive Income Podcast.

4. Online Communities – Online communities are a great way to connect with other solopreneurs and small business owners. You can join groups on Facebook,

LinkedIn, and Reddit to network, share ideas and learn from others. You can also find niche-specific communities that focus on your industry, providing you with relevant insights and resources.

5. Blogs and Websites – There are several blogs and websites that offer valuable insights and resources for solopreneurs. You can find blogs on different niches, including entrepreneurship, marketing, and technology. Some popular blogs for solopreneurs include The Solopreneur Hour, Chris Ducker, and Smart Passive Income.

In conclusion, as a solopreneur, you must continue to learn and grow to remain competitive in the digital world. Fortunately, there are several resources available to help you continue your growth and learning. Online courses, webinars, podcasts, online communities, blogs, and websites are all great resources that you can explore to continue your learning journey.

www.ingramcontent.com/pod-product-compliance
Lightning Source LLC
Chambersburg PA
CBHW070849220526
45466CB00005B/1941